D0773672

Weather

Lynn Huggins-Cooper

Illustrated by
Shelagh McNicholas and David Burroughs

A⁺
Smart Apple Media

First published in 2003 by Franklin Watts
96 Leonard Street, London EC2A 4XD

Franklin Watts Australia
45-51 Huntley Street
Alexandria, NSW 2015

Series editor: Rachel Cooke
Art director: Jonathan Hair
Design: James Marks

Published in the United States by Smart Apple Media
1980 Lookout Drive, North Mankato, Minnesota 56003

Library of Congress Cataloging-in-Publication Data

Huggins-Cooper, Lynn.
Weather / Lynn Huggins-Cooper ; illustrated by Shelagh
McNicholas, David Burroughs.
p. cm. — (First-hand science)
Includes index.
Summary: A young boy experiences daily changes in the
weather. Facts about the weather and meteorology and
questions for the reader are interspersed throughout the text.
ISBN 1-58340-445-7
1. Meteorology—Juvenile literature. 2. Weather—Juvenile
literature. [1. Weather. 2. Meteorology.] I. McNicholas,
Shelagh, ill. II. Burroughs, David, ill. III. Title.

QC863.5.H54 2004
551.5—dc22   2003058971

9 8 7 6 5 4 3 2 1

Contents

Joe likes to play outside—whatever the weather. Come and join him!

What's the weather like?

Every day when Joe gets up, he looks out of the window. What's the weather going to be like today?

Here are some different kinds of weather:

Rainy

Sunny

Windy

Snowy

What's the weather like today where you are?

It's a warm, sunny day. Joe and his mom are going on a picnic! What will Joe choose to wear?

When it's hot, we wear clothes that help us keep cool, such as shorts and T-shirts.

When it's cold, we wear warm sweaters and jackets.

Is it always warm when it's sunny? Would you wear shorts and a T-shirt on a sunny day in winter?

Joe enjoys his picnic. He thinks his dark glasses and hat look funny!

How is Joe protected from the sun?

The **sun** gives us heat. We have to be careful, though—the sun can burn our skin and make it red and sore. These things protect us from sunburn:

Sun hats

Sunblock

Loose T-shirt with sleeves

Dark glasses to protect our eyes from bright sunlight

8

During the day, the sun gives us light. If something blocks the sunlight, it casts shadows.

At night, when the sun sets, it gets dark. We use electric lights to see by.

Mom sits under the tree. She likes it because it is cool and shady.

Never look straight at the sun—even with dark glasses on! The bright light can hurt your eyes.

Kite weather

The wind has started to blow. Joe and his mom are flying a kite. The wind carries it high in the air!

How can Joe tell which way the wind is blowing?

Wind is moving air.

Cold winds blow from cold places—such as the snowy **Poles**.

Hot winds blow from hot places—such as a baking **desert**.

10

The wind has brought some clouds. Joe likes spotting animal shapes in them.

Clouds are made from tiny water droplets in the air.

Sometimes, water falls from the clouds as **rain**.

Rainwater collects in rivers, lakes, and the sea. Some of it rises up into the air again as an invisible gas. High in the sky, the gas turns back into water droplets.

???

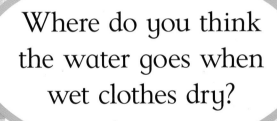

Where do you think the water goes when wet clothes dry?

It's raining

Now the clouds have hidden the sun. It looks gray and dark. Soon it starts to rain.

Inside the clouds, water droplets join together.

The drops get too big and heavy and fall out of the sky—as rain!

Joe loves jumping in puddles. What clothes would he need for a walk in the rain?

Joe and Mom have found somewhere to shelter. The sun is trying to come out again!

Look, Mom! A rainbow!

Rainbows happen when sunlight shines through raindrops. The white sunlight breaks up into different colors—and we see a rainbow!

We see seven colors in rainbows.

red orange yellow green blue indigo violet

Making plants grow

Joe and Mom go home. The rain has stopped. Water droplets glitter everywhere. The plants won't need watering tonight!

My tomatoes are coming along nicely.

These apples look ripe.

Plants need light and water to grow properly.

Plants grow year-round—
but different things grow
in different **seasons**.

In autumn, the
leaves turn brown
and blow away.

As summer ends,
the fruit is ripe
and ready to eat.

Are there any fruits
or vegetables that you
eat in the summer
but not in the winter?

In winter, the
apple tree's
branches are bare.

The fruit grows
larger through the
warm summer.

The blossom petals
drop off, leaving
behind tiny fruit.

In spring, the tree
blossoms and its
leaves unfurl.

Stormy weather

Joe's playing indoors today. A storm rages outside. Thunder rumbles and lightning flashes.

Very strong winds blow during a **storm**. Use the pictures to see how windy it is outside today!

Calm: the trees are still.

Gentle breeze: leaves rustle.

Fresh breeze: branches sway and leaves blow around.

16

Storms can be dangerous, but Joe knows he is safe indoors. Cleo, his cat, is not so sure!

The storm will go away soon, Cleo.

Stay safe in a thunderstorm—inside a house or in a car.

Don't stay under a tree, because **lightning** could strike it.

Gale: twigs and branches may break off trees.

Hurricane: very strong wind that can blow down trees and houses!

You usually hear **thunder** after you see lightning. The closer the storm, the less time there is between the lightning and the thunder.

17

Hail!

The storm is getting noisy now! Joe listens to hail drumming on the roof.

Water falls to the ground in lots of different ways.

Sometimes it "spits"—and only a few drops fall.

Sometimes it drizzles. The raindrops are tiny and light.

Sometimes it pours with rain.

Sometimes, in stormy weather, **hail** falls. Water droplets freeze high in the sky. They fall to the ground as chunks of **ice** or hailstones.

Mom has collected some hailstones in a dish. They look like little white peas!

Sometimes, in cold weather, **snow** falls.

In some parts of the world, hailstones can be huge—and dangerous! In really bad storms, they can be bigger than tennis balls.

Snow is made in the clouds when water droplets freeze around a tiny piece of dust.

If you look at snowflakes with a magnifier, you see many different and beautiful shapes. But they all have six sides, or points!

Snow and ice

Joe and Mom are talking about the snow last winter. They remember how Joe built a snowcat.

Snow falls only when it is cold. We usually see snow during the winter.

Some mountains are so high that they are always cold and always covered in snow and ice.

Joe loves snow! He likes to lie down and flap his arms and legs in it. When he gets up, he's made a "snow angel."

When it's very cold, snowflakes are small and powdery. When it's a little warmer, the flakes are larger—like fluffy white feathers!

21

Joe and Mom also remember one day when it was cold and frosty. Everything was white and glittered in the sunshine.

Frost happens after clear, cold nights. Water droplets on the ground, on plants, and on spiders' webs freeze into ice.

If it stays cold for a while, long needles of frost are made. This is called hoarfrost.

Have you ever woken up and seen the grass covered in frost? What do you remember about it?

Ice is frozen water. It is solid and cannot flow.

Icicles form where dripping water freezes.

When it gets warmer, the ice begins to melt, and the icicles drip slowly away.

Icicles hung from the roof, and the pond was frozen solid. Joe was careful not to slip and fall down.

Water changes to ice when it gets cold. What happens when water is heated? Look back at page 11 for a clue.

23

Weather watch

The storm is over at last. Joe has made his own weather station. Mom is helping him collect information.

Scientists collect all sorts of information to study the weather. They try to discover what the weather will be like tomorrow, next week, or next month.

They measure how much rain falls.

What is Joe doing to watch the weather?

They measure
the temperature
—how hot it is.

They use **satellites**
in space to see how
clouds and air are
moving around our planet.

They check the
strength of the wind
and where it is
coming from.

We see their results when
we watch the **weather
forecast** on television.

25

All sorts of weather

Joe enjoys all sorts
of weather!

Hail

Rain

? ? ?

What season
do you think each
photo is showing? How
can you tell?

Snow

Frost and ice

In what weather would Joe use the things below? Can you spot them in his photographs?

Fog

Sunshine

Wind

kite

ice skates

wooly gloves, hat, and scarf

flashlight

rubber boots

umbrella

sun hat

Try this yourself

Have some weather fun!

Weather watching

Today, there are lots of scientific ways of forecasting the weather. In the past, people used seaweed and pinecones to decide if rain was on the way. Find a pinecone or some seaweed and try it for yourself.

If the spines on the pinecone are closed, it means the air is damp—and it may rain. If the spines are open, the air is dry, and it will be a fine day!

If the seaweed feels dry and crispy, it will be a dry, sunny day.

If the seaweed feels rubbery, it might rain!

Cloud gazing

On a day when the clouds are broken up and fluffy, try Joe's game of spotting shapes in them (see page 11). Now paint a picture using the cloud shape as a starting point.

The right clothes

The clothes these people are wearing are just right for the weather in their part of the world.

Why do you think this woman's outfit is good for the cold Poles?

Why do you think this man's outfit is good in the hot desert?

Design your own outfits for different kinds of weather—one for hot weather and one for cold weather.

Useful words

clouds: Water droplets massed together in the air.

desert: A very dry place where few plants grow.

fog: A kind of cloud that forms close to the ground.

frost: When water on the surface of things such as plants freezes.

hail: Chunks of ice that sometimes fall in a storm.

ice: Frozen water.

lightning: Electric flashes made by some storms.

Poles: The far north and south of Earth where it is always cold and icy.

rain: Water that falls from clouds.

satellites: Machines sent into space to circle and watch Earth.

seasons: The different times of year—spring, summer, autumn, and winter—with their own types of weather.

snow: The frozen flakes of ice that fall in cold weather.

storm: Very windy and often very wet weather.

sun: Our nearest star. It gives us heat and light.

thunder: The noise made when lightning flashes.

weather forecast: Saying what the weather will be like in the future.

weather station: A place where information about the weather is collected.

wind: Moving air.

About this book

This book encourages children to explore and discover science in their local, familiar environment—in the garden or at the park. By starting from "where they are," it aims to increase children's knowledge and understanding of the world around them, encouraging them to examine the natural world and its processes closely and from a more scientific perspective.

The weather is explored, focusing on its daily changes and linking it to the seasons. Questions are asked to build on children's natural curiosity and encourage them to think about what they are reading. Some questions send children back to the book to find the answers, others point to new ideas that, through discussion, the readers may "discover" for themselves.

Index